Original title:
The House of Quiet Reflection

Copyright © 2025 Creative Arts Management OÜ
All rights reserved.

Author: Helena Marchant
ISBN HARDBACK: 978-1-80587-134-7
ISBN PAPERBACK: 978-1-80587-604-5

The Calm Between Heartbeats

In a corner, silence snickers,
As life outside just flickers.
The clock's tick-tock takes a nap,
While I enjoy my cosmic wrap.

A cat on a cushion sighs wide,
Joking how we all abide.
With tea that seems to laugh and sing,
I ponder what tomorrow brings.

A Retreat from the Clamor

Noise takes a stroll, I swear,
As I sit with my comfy chair.
The walls hold whispers, oh so sly,
While I nibble on a piece of pie.

Books pile high, like jokes untold,
Each word a giggle, crisp and bold.
Who needs a show when inside's so bright?
I start a dance in the dimmest light.

Still Waters Run Deep

In ponds of thought where ducks debate,
I giggle at my pondered fate.
Reflections wink with playful glee,
As frogs recite their philosophy.

Ripples of laughter chase the gloom,
Water lilies dance in full bloom.
Time takes a break for what it's worth,
As I crack jokes about the earth.

The Unfolding of Time's Embrace

Time sprawls out like an idle cat,
Pretending it's too cool to chat.
Seconds tick along with flair,
While I just lounge, with time to spare.

A calendar that grins on the wall,
Says every day's a comedy hall.
So here I sit in timeless bliss,
Pranking myself with a blissful hiss.

Shadows Beneath the Eaves

In corners where dust bunnies dare,
A cat knocks over a chair.
Socks are missing, no one knows why,
And laundry flirts like it might fly.

The spider spins a web of cheer,
In hopes of catching a passing tear.
The clock ticks loudly, just for fun,
As mice dance under the muted sun.

A ghost in slippers might sneak by,
With a playful wink and a sly sigh.
Echoes of laughter from ages past,
Make the quiet moments unsurpassed.

Yet in the stillness, we find delight,
As shadows whisper in the night.
Beneath the eaves, our secrets hide,
Where silliness and silence collide.

The Hushed Corners of Memory

In the nook where old chairs recline,
Echoes of giggles intertwine.
A teacup rings, it spills the tea,
While cookies run off wild and free.

The clock insists on counting time,
But what's the hurry? Life's a rhyme.
With every tick, a secret shared,
In whispered tones, no one is scared.

Old books sigh with stories hid,
Of mischief managed, a kid who slid.
In shadowed corners, joy awaits,
With silly games and playful fates.

The memories squeak, dance about,
In hushed tones, they laugh and shout.
While silliness colors every thought,
In this sanctuary, laughter is caught.

Reveries in a Gentle Dawn

The coffee brews with a cheerful tune,
As spoons perform a lively swoon.
Fluffy pancakes stack their claim,
While syrup drips like a golden rain.

The sunlight peeks through the pane,
To find a cat who's lost its brain.
Chasing shadows, it leaps high,
As birds burst forth with a morning cry.

A breeze hums tunes that never tire,
As curtains dance near the fire.
With every breath, a giggle swells,
In this lovely home where joy dwells.

From sleepy corners, chuckles rise,
In the gentle light, there are no lies.
Each dawn a canvas, bright and clear,
For laughter's echo to persevere.

Soft Footfalls on Dusty Floors

With each footfall, dust puffs fly,
Older than time, it waves goodbye.
In slippers shuffling, giggles ignite,
As shadows tango in morning light.

The floorboards creak a silly song,
Reminding everyone, they don't belong.
Each little squeak tells a tale,
Of secret meetings and a hidden trail.

The chairs are full of whispered cheer,
While mismatched socks disappear.
A brave light flickers, a warm embrace,
In this place where we find our grace.

As dust motes swirl in the sun's beam,
We share our dreams in a silenced scream.
Soft footfalls scatter without a care,
In the joyous echoes that fill the air.

Solitary Gaze

In a corner sat a cat,
Eyes like marbles, looking fat.
He judged the world through glassy stare,
As if to say, "I'm quite aware."

A snail slid by, slowest of all,
The cat just yawned, didn't care at all.
"Why rush?" he thought, "It's all a daze,
Just me and my nap in a sunlit blaze."

Twilight Thoughts

As shadows stretch and birds take flight,
The gnomes begin their dance at night.
With floppy hats and clumsy feet,
They twirl around, a silly feat.

The moon snickers, up so high,
Doubling over as gnome heads fly.
Laughter spills from wooden lips,
As they all take their clumsy trips.

Embrace of Quietude

A frog once claimed, with a ribbit loud,
"I've pondered life, and I'm quite proud."
Then slipped on a leaf, quite out of style,
Sending crickets into a giggling pile.

With every splash, he lost his grace,
Yet wore that smile across his face.
"Who needs fancy," he did croak,
"When being silly is the best folk joke?"

Shaded Peace

Beneath a tree, a tortoise naps,
Dreaming of races, and maybe some traps.
But lo and behold, just in his dreams,
A rabbit loses by silent screams.

He wakes with a grin, no hurry today,
While squirrels gossip in the leafy ballet.
"Take your time!" he calls with glee,
"Life's a race, but what's the fee?"

The Quiet Beneath

In a nook where silence breathes,
Dust bunnies swirl beneath the eaves.
A cat sits atop a velvet chair,
Pretending to be the king of air.

Socks vanish with a playful grin,
Each pair a mystery held within.
Tea kisses steam in a laughter trace,
While books conspire in their own space.

Chairs giggle, creak with a sigh,
They've witnessed secrets, you and I.
The clock chimes twice, then skips a beat,
As if it's chuckling at our seat.

A window cracks with a witty breeze,
Tickling the curtains, bringing ease.
This realm of cheer, where shadows play,
Turns ordinary moments into a ballet.

Serenity's Canvas

With splashes of calm in every hue,
Walls whisper stories, old and new.
A brush of light twirls its golden thread,
Painting laughter where silence is spread.

Cushions collide in a marshmallow brawl,
As plump pillows rise and take the fall.
Spilled tea morphs into a comedy scene,
Sipping chaos like it's a cuisine.

Lamps giggle softly, shed a bright grin,
Illuminating secrets trapped within.
Who knew such peace could crack a joke,
As echoes of chuckles swiftly evoke?

A canvas of calm where shadows compose,
Every creak and sigh, in laughs they propose.
This is a place where the stillness rewrites,
Turning silence into delightful delights.

Quiet Sessions of the Heart

In a chamber where whispers tickle the air,
Dreams dance lightly without a care.
Puddles of stillness hold giggles inside,
As echoes of joy take a rhythm and glide.

A teapot chuckles, steam curling high,
As biscuits play hide-and-seek nearby.
Each clink and clatter, a symphony grand,
Filling the corners of this cozy land.

Socks swing by, joining in on the fun,
This is where quiet becomes a pun.
They tease at the squishy, comfy old rug,
While blankets give in to a cozy hug.

With every sigh, a giggle resounds,
Tickling the silence in waves and bounds.
This heart of calm whispers loud and clear,
Making solitude a place to cheer.

The Whisper of Shadows

Shadows waltz in the twilight glow,
Leading the fun where few dare go.
A couch hums softly, joined by a sneeze,
As laughter erupts with the greatest of ease.

The chandelier jingles, a clumsy ballet,
While critters plot mischief in the fray.
Giggling walls overhear a light tale,
As whispers drift like a breezy sail.

Every nook hides a curious mouse,
Scheming and dreaming about the house.
They sip on the stillness, giggling in cue,
Turning mundane moments to something new.

Embracing shadows, we savor the night,
With chuckles that twinkle, oh what a sight!
In this realm where silence sings loud,
Laughter weaves magic, painting us proud.

Harbor of Introspection

In corners where thoughts begin to dance,
A sock's lost partner takes a chance.
The cat meows with a serious face,
As if pondering life's curious race.

A teapot whistles a silly song,
Echoing dreams where we all belong.
The couch giggles under my weight,
As if teasing my procrastinate fate.

Old magazines play hide and seek,
While dust bunnies gather, quite unique.
A clock ticks loud, or is it me?
Time's a jester, laughing with glee.

In quiet corners, laughter brews,
With every silence, a joke ensues.
In this retreat where thinking's a sport,
Even solitude finds joy, well-caught!

Peaceful Portals

Behind the door, a joke awaits,
A sandwich whispers, 'Don't clean your plates!'
The mirror chuckles with every glance,
Reflecting the awkwardness of circumstance.

A plant's advice is hard to take,
'Grow tall, be wise!'—but it's a fake.
The lamp blinks twice, what's the deal?
Is it trying to flirt, or just reel?

Chairs chatter, sharing their woes,
While the dust settles like forgotten prose.
The rug rolls its eyes, boredom's its fate,
Wishing for more than just a mute state.

In calm silence, hints of jest,
Where thoughts are goofy, and no one's stressed.
In hidden nooks with smiles, oh so bright,
Even silence can sparkle with delight!

Tranquility's Tapestry

The walls paint stories, with every shade,
Of noodle noodles and lemonade.
A chair snores softly, dreams on its own,
While the bookshelf giggles at tales overgrown.

A clock spins yarns, oh so absurd,
'Time flies by like a silly bird!'
Each room grins, a sarcastic show,
Even silence knows when it should grow.

A spork in the drawer, quite out of place,
Claims it's a hero of mealtime grace.
In midst of tranquility, chaos can leap,
With laughter as secrets, they're ours to keep.

In cozy corners, chuckles arise,
As winks float softly, sweet surprise.
With every gaze, a funny scene,
In this woven world, all feels serene!

Woven Threads of Solitude

Empty rooms where echoes tease,
The fridge hums jokes over cheese.
A picture frame prefers its fate,
Staring at me, with judgment, it waits.

Socks conspire, plotting their flight,
While the curtains sway, dancing in spite.
The rug shakes dust, with utmost grace,
As mismatched slippers join in the race.

An old hat tips, it's seen it all,
Whispering tales of spring and fall.
The air's thick with secrets shared,
While the stoves plot meals they never dared.

In threads of laughter, solace is spun,
A private theater, where life is fun.
Each quiet moment, a punchline waits,
In solitude, where the absurd creates!

Pathways to Inner Light

In corners where dust bunnies leap,
Whispers of thoughts quietly creep.
Each room a stage, a comic show,
Where socks play hide and giggles flow.

The chair's got secrets, just ask it twice,
It'll spill the tea, oh, so precise.
The clock ticks slow, with comic flair,
Time laughs at worries, if you dare.

A tumbleweed rolls across the floor,
Chasing the laughter, it wants more.
With echoes of jest in every nook,
Each shadow's a friend with jokes to cook.

The light spills in, like syrup so sweet,
Bouncing off walls with a rhythmic beat.
A world of smiles in every glance,
Where silliness leads the heart to dance.

Sanctuary of the Unvoiced

In corners where silence sprinkles cheer,
Mismatched curtains wiggle near.
A couch that giggles, soft and plush,
It swallows all worries with a hush.

Plants roll their leaves in leafy debates,
Chatting with dust motes about their fates.
The fridge hums jokes, a cooler delight,
As leftovers dance under the soft light.

Candles flicker, stifling a snort,
While rugs weave tales of the clowns they sport.
With echoes of laughter bouncing away,
This refuge of quiet welcomes play.

Mirrors reflect the jester in you,
Turning solemn thoughts to zany hues.
With giggles that sip from teacups so bright,
Serenity blooms in laughter's light.

Soft Hues of Reflection

In the stillness, where chuckles collide,
Pillows hold secrets they cannot hide.
Walls blush in hues of coral and jade,
As quirky reflections make the grade.

The cat nearly chortles at its own tail,
While curtains conspire in a fluttering gale.
A book on the shelf whispers tales of glee,
Adventures where socks can float like a tree.

In puddles of sunlight, silliness gleams,
Inviting the world to follow dreams.
Nooks filled with giggles, a warm embrace,
Become a stage for laughter's race.

From shadows that dance to whispers that yawn,
This space springs new life at the crack of dawn.
Every moment, a canvas so bright,
Drawn with the hues of pure delight.

In the Fold of Silence

Within these walls, where stillness reigns,
Whimsical echoes transcend the pains.
A sock puppet party on the table,
Each cheery face, ready and able.

The floorboards creak with ancient mirth,
Turning silence into joyous birth.
A ticklish logic lingers nearby,
As the bookshelf mumbles a witty reply.

Candles quirk when a breeze sneaks through,
Swaying in laughter as shadows grew.
Sofas lounge in their lazy delight,
Sharing secrets with all who invite.

In the fold of whispers, let joy awake,
As mismatched spoons dance and shake.
A warm embrace in this playful space,
Laughter and peace gently interlace.

Stillness in Motion

In a room where echoes play,
Chairs do waltz, night and day.
The clocks giggle, tickle the air,
Time's a prank with a quirky flair.

Cats hold council, tails held high,
Debating naps as clouds drift by.
Sunbeams scatter with feline grace,
Whiskers twitch in this quiet space.

Socks in corners, socks on shelves,
Dare to sit and talk to themselves.
A chair spins tales of starlit dreams,
While shadows plot out mischievous schemes.

In this stillness, the fun unfurls,
Laughter dances, twirls, and swirls.
A silent ruckus, a peaceful spree,
In every corner, a joke's set free.

Fables of the Quiet Mind

In a tranquil nook where no one fights,
Dreams leap freely, take to heights.
Clouds tell tales with whispers bright,
Fluttering words of pure delight.

Teacups giggle as saucers spin,
In this realm, chaotic kin.
A wise old book with bent dog-ear,
Teaches parables only dogs hear.

The mirror laughs as it bends and bows,
Reflecting squirrels in all their prowse.
Each quiet chuckle, a gentle tease,
As laughter bobs like leaves in the breeze.

Fables flutter, in soft reprieve,
In this quiet, nonsense we believe.
With every sigh, giggles unwind,
Tales of splendor, all intertwined.

Unraveling Silence

In corridors where whispers sleep,
Lurking secrets begin to creep.
A crumpled note, a laugh in the air,
Puzzles spin with a funny flair.

The couch reclines with utmost pride,
Holding secrets it can't confide.
Pillows gossip, trade silly quips,
As laughter bubbles, and silence slips.

Light spills softly, a lazy cat,
Stretched like a Fabel with a hat.
Lampshades giggle under soft glow,
Sharing tales of the sofa's woe.

Even the dust has stories to tell,
Of how it endured, quite well.
In this void where giggles blend,
Every silence is a laughter's friend.

Haunted by Peace

In a cozy nook, shadows sneak,
Turning whispers into a peek.
A flickering light, a chuckle aloof,
Creaking wood gives an old ghost proof.

Candles debate who flickers best,
While the curtains play a game of jest.
Lurking spirits sip on tea,
Dancing politely, timelessly free.

Chairs gossip of the ghostly past,
Remembering a time with shadows cast.
Serene laughter floats through the hall,
A quiet party, inviting all.

In stillness, a giggle rides the breeze,
Echoing softly among the trees.
A playful peace, a cheeky cheer,
In this realm, all are welcome here.

A Canvas of Peaceful Absence

In a room where silence thrives,
Dust bunnies dance like wild jives.
The cat naps on a cushion high,
Dreaming of fish that float on by.

A chair that creaks with every sigh,
Whispers secrets, oh so sly.
The clock ticks softly, time takes bends,
As laughter floats on air, it blends.

A vase of flowers in a trance,
Wishes of bees, they prance and prance.
The window frames a gentle view,
Where squirrels debate on what to pursue.

In this space, the chaos still,
A crooked frame with slight goodwill.
Funny how nothing feels amiss,
In moments where tranquility's bliss.

Among the Stillness, I Bloom.

In corners flat where shadows spread,
A geranium grins, it can't be wed.
A goldfish giggles behind glass walls,
While autumn leaves entertain their falls.

I tiptoe in for a visit quick,
Among the calm, my heart does kick.
A bunny fumbles at the door,
Wants to share tales of folklore.

No meetings here, just time to play,
With imaginary friends all day.
Through whispered thoughts and paper cranes,
I dance with joy in gentle rains.

The silence chats in playful tones,
Among the quiet, I find my zones.
In this soft laugh of time's expanse,
I bloom and twirl, in a merry dance.

Whispers of Stillness

A teapot whistles a curvy tune,
While moths debate the light of the moon.
A rug with patterns of ancient lore,
Catches laughter like dust on the floor.

Frogs in the garden sing bass parades,
While shadows waltz in sunlit glades.
A couch with cushions of dreams and schemes,
Offers repose to a land of beams.

The echo of footsteps tries to flee,
Chasing the whispers of a bumblebee.
Even the curtains are full of cheer,
As they dance along, the day draws near.

In this space where all seems right,
Funny how shadows can bring delight.
With every chime and brief embrace,
Stillness smiles, oh what a place!

Echoes in the alcove

In the alcove where echoes coo,
A chair delays, 'I'll wait for you!'
The wallpaper giggles with each glance,
As dust motes join in a sunlit dance.

A book lies open, its pages fanned,
Holding stories from a far-off land.
The clock gives nods like it's in on jest,
While silence throws a lighthearted fest.

Socks in the dryer tumble and play,
Joking about how bright they may stay.
An old guitar plays a soft refrain,
Strumming the chords that drive us sane.

Echoes linger like a joke retold,
In this alcove, nothing gets old.
With laughter sprinkled through the air,
Fun hides within this quiet lair.

The Warmth of Lingering Shadows

In corners where the dust bunnies play,
A sofa whispers secrets of the day.
The cat on the mantle dreams of a mouse,
While goldfish gossip about their small house.

The clock is stuck; it's laughable, indeed,
Time takes a nap while we wander with speed.
A painting winks, it's seen better days,
It's a masterpiece in a very weird way.

The cobwebs sway like dancers in flight,
To old tunes humming softly through the night.
Every creak of the floor holds a chuckle,
Like it's saying, 'Hey, do you hear that chuckle?'

Between shadows, we linger and laugh,
In this whimsical, wobbly photograph.
Life moves forward, but here we just rest,
In the warm embrace of the shadowy jest.

Gazing at the Unseen

Behind the door labeled 'Do Not Peek',
Lies a world where imaginations tweak.
Dust motes waltz in the beams of the sun,
While I swear I heard a rhythmic hum.

The chairs have a meeting, no humans in sight,
Discussing their dreams of taking a flight.
A banana in the bowl dreams of pie,
While curtains roll their eyes with a sigh.

The rug tells tall tales of shoes long gone,
Each thread a story spun from dusk till dawn.
I grab a cookie, thinking it's rough,
But it's been waiting patiently, all tough.

The room holds its breath, waiting for a cue,
For the invisible audience to give a "Woo!"
Yet, all that I find is the sound of my snack,
As I gaze at the unseen, I give a wink back.

Pieces of Yesterday's Light

Caught in a jar, a firefly's glow,
Thinking it's great, but it really doesn't know.
A sunbeam slumps on the edge of the chair,
Its fate is to linger with a rusted despair.

Spectacles sit proudly, collecting some dust,
While memories swirl 'round like a musty old bust.
The faint scent of cake somehow hangs in the air,
While I try to recall when I baked with flair.

The wallpaper chuckles at stories once told,
Faded dreams in the patterns, bold yet cold.
A light bulb flickers like it's aging with grace,
Revealing the humor hidden in space.

Here we sit, slicing through time with delight,
Pieces of yesterday's light out of sight.
Laughing at ghosts, we share lots of cheer,
In this playful arena where nothing's unclear.

The Poetry of Empty Spaces

In the quiet where echoes chase their tail,
I find the charm in tales that are stale.
Vacant chairs hold court, offering a seat,
To fill up the voids with giggles and heat.

An empty bowl holds yesterday's feast,
It chuckles, 'I promise I'm not a beast!'
The silence is loud; oh, what a conundrum,
As shadows join hands and dance to a hum.

Walls carry whispers of jokes long since shared,
In corners, the memories linger and dared.
The space in between us plays hide-and-seek,
Even the dust seems to hold back a peek.

So here we roam in this zany retreat,
The poetry of empty spaces is sweet.
With laughter and jests, we fill every crack,
In this whimsical lair, we never hold back.

Asylum of the Aether

In a space where thoughts often play,
Mice wear hats, prance in a ballet.
Couches whisper secrets bold,
And tea turns into stories told.

Light bulbs giggle at the night,
As shadows dance with sheer delight.
Coffee cups hold gossip grand,
And fish join in a rock band.

Chairs trade jokes without a care,
While books conspire in a lair.
Footprints walk in backward style,
And laughter echoes for a mile.

In this realm of silly dreams,
Nothing's ever as it seems.
A delightfully odd retreat,
Where weird and funny always meet.

Retreat into Stillness

In a nook where quiet likes to hide,
Cats take naps, their paws astride.
Bottles chuckle, rolling around,
And silence sings without a sound.

Pillows plot and hats conspire,
While curtains sway in laughter's choir.
Jars of pickles form a pact,
To buy a yacht with plans intact.

The clock ticks slow, but time goes fast,
As whispers swirl, a merry blast.
Stillness plays a goofy tune,
And crickets join the fun at noon.

In this zone of subtle bliss,
Every moment's filled with a fizz.
With giggles dancing on a whim,
Laughter bubbles to the brim.

The Silence Within

Inside the quiet, jesters dwell,
Whiskers twitch, and secrets swell.
Silence wears a clownish hat,
While echoes play with a cheeky cat.

Thoughts sit down for tea and cake,
Discussing if a chair can shake.
Echoes tease and whispers hum,
In a world where nonsense comes.

Walls are painted with light banter,
While corners hold a laughter mantra.
Shadows giggle, shadows quake,
As sunbeams laugh for goodness' sake.

In every corner, silliness kneels,
While laughter turns into a wheel.
Moments pause, then burst with cheer,
In this silence, humor's near.

Gallery of Mindful Murmurs

A gallery filled with chuckles bright,
Painted whispers, swirls of light.
Frames of thoughts hang on the wall,
As laughter echoes through the hall.

Each canvas spills a blend of glee,
Where ticklish voices float like a bee.
Footsteps dance on cotton fluff,
In this place where light gets rough.

Socks gossip in a joyful spree,
While moths debate on what to be.
Windows blink with mirthful surprise,
As ribbons peek with curious eyes.

In every inch, a whimsy tale,
While shadows join a playful gale.
A gallery where laughter's king,
And quiet's just a silly fling.

Whispers in the Stillness

In corners where dust bunnies roam,
And socks surely seek a new home.
The cat yawns wide, a royal decree,
That napping's best, just wait and see.

Silent giggles behind closet doors,
Where socks dance wild on polished floors.
Every chair seems to whisper a tale,
Of crumbs and spills, and a missing nail.

The clock ticks slow, a tortoise in race,
With time for tea and a nap's embrace.
A miming ghost haunts the hallway bright,
Made of dust, but it swears it's light.

In shadows where the echoes laugh,
You'll find the secrets of a lazy path.
So join the fun in this sleepy maze,
Where peace and jest find time to play.

Echoes of Solitude

In the corner stands a plump old chair,
With a cushion that's lost its initial flair.
It creaks and groans, can't hold its peace,
While a ghost of a snack calls for release.

The tea kettle whistles a silly old tune,
As the fridge hums bass, like a funky cartoon.
A paperclip orchestra starts to play,
In this realm where boredom sways away.

Pictures hang crooked, gossiping old frames,
While forgotten socks play silly old games.
The rug yawns wide, a comfortable zone,
Where mismatched thoughts feel right at home.

So here we linger in quirky delight,
With echoes of laughter and whispers of night.
Join the parade of the odd and the free,
In solitude's home, we find harmony.

Lanterns in the Gloaming

When dusk settles with a wink and a grin,
The moths gather round, dancing skin to skin.
Lanterns flicker like giggles in air,
As fireflies join the evening's affair.

Creaky doors send a chuckle or two,
While the furniture hums a raucous view.
A game of hide and seek, quite absurd,
With the broom as a friend, not a word heard.

Cobwebs wave like ribbons in breeze,
Where laughter hangs low, and worries freeze.
The sock drawer opens to whisper a plan,
Of a sock revolution, led by a man.

So let's raise a toast, with cups filled with cheer,
To lanterns that giggle through the shadowy sphere.
In this twilight realm of silly play,
We find joy in the gloaming, day after day.

A Sanctuary of Silence

In a nook where echoes of humor lie,
Where even the silence seems to sigh.
A plant in the corner does yoga and bends,
While the candlestick wiggles, making amends.

Under the pot where the dust bunnies dwell,
A squirrel writes tales, as quiet as a shell.
With teacups clanking in a learned dance,
This sanctuary offers a whimsical chance.

Old slippers converse about paths they've tread,
While the ceiling spins yarns overhead.
The curtains flap in a playful zany way,
Swaying to melodies, they, too, want to play.

So welcome to laughter in folds soft and round,
Where silence and whimsy are equally found.
In this haven where chuckles take flight,
We cherish the stillness, and all feels just right.

Sanctuary of the Soul

In a nook with a chair that's too plush,
Socks on the carpet, I lounge in a rush.
Coffee in hand, and a cat on my lap,
Wondering how I fell into this trap.

Dust bunnies dance to an old tune,
While the clock ticks softly, it's nearly noon.
The fridge is a treasure, but I fear the smell,
As I dream of a meal—too hungry to dwell.

Cushions surround me like hugs from the past,
Memories linger, they never go fast.
With laughter and echoes from corners unseen,
This place is a haven, both silly and green.

So here's to the quirks of my cozy retreat,
Where nothing's too silly, nothing's too neat.
In the sanctuary found just behind the door,
I chuckle at life and just wish for more.

Veiled Thoughts

In a corner where whispers can't reach,
I ponder my life like a lesson from teach.
With a hat on my head and dreams in my pocket,
I plan my escape from the mundane rocket.

Puddles of sunlight spill on the floor,
I dive into thought, though I land on the snore.
Birds chirp a tune that I barely remember,
Is it springtime or maybe just September?

A cushion retreats as I ponder my fate,
Is it too late for this mind of a great?
I sketch out the stars, and they giggle at me,
A stellar performance of cosmic debris.

Oh, nooks full of veils, where thoughts drift like mist,
I wrap them in laughter, can't let them be missed.
With a wink and a smile, these visions unfold,
In this comedy show, I'm the star, I'm bold.

Nooks of Contemplation

Where cushions collide in a fluffy embrace,
I ponder my world in a slow, lumpy race.
The kettle sings secrets, a whistle so bright,
Awaiting my sips while I ponder the night.

In nooks where my thoughts love to creep and to crawl,
I trip on the playlist of my very own thrall.
Jokes to be told, and adventures to brew,
Under the lamp that is slightly askew.

Shoes in a pile, like a sleepy parade,
I kick off my worries, let the jokes cascade.
The clock starts to chuckle, and I can't help but grin,
As I plot out my dreams with a playful spin.

Laughter still echoes in the crevices deep,
While I nap in the corner or maybe I creep.
In these nooks of reflection, profound and absurd,
I find that true wisdom is often unheard.

Chamber of Dreams

Step into a chamber where chaos is king,
With cushions that giggle and curtains that sing.
A banana-shaped lamp casts shadows so weird,
While I chase my dreams with a snack that's not feared.

Clouds of old laughter float high in the air,
Each giggle a riddle, a delightful affair.
The floor creaks a tune as I shuffle around,
Waltzing with memories that jump off the ground.

Pajamas my armor, I brace for the night,
In this chamber of dreams where absurd takes flight.
My bedtime stories are wrapped up in fun,
As I battle my pillows, pretending to run.

With giggles and grins, the moon dips down low,
In this chamber of whimsy, I let my heart glow.
So here's to the nights when the dreams drift and play,
In the laughter-filled shadows, they're never far away.

Mindful Niche

In a cozy nook with a cat on my lap,
I ponder my snacks while I take a nap.
Dust bunnies dance, quite the quirky view,
They've got better rhythm than I ever do.

The chair squeaks loud, a symphony strange,
Echoing thoughts that refuse to change.
A sock puppets plays on the armrest's edge,
Claiming the spotlight, oh how it dreads!

Tea brews a tale of spilled mischief and fun,
While I sprawl on the couch like a shipwrecked one.
The clock softly chimes, declaring a break,
From seriousness, laughter is all I can make.

So here in my niche, all worries take flight,
With giggles and snacks, it just feels so right.
The world outside shouts, but in here it's grand,
A quirky retreat made just as I planned.

Hidden Harmonies

In the corner, the plants hum a bees' tune,
While snoring dog dreams of chasing the moon.
The lamp flickers sparks like a lighthearted joke,
As shadows join in, they dance and they poke.

A cup of warm coffee wears a whipped cream crown,
While socks on the floor seem to laugh with a frown.
The fridge softly sighs, full of leftover cheer,
If only it spoke, we'd have quite the seer.

I play hide and seek with my overflowing thoughts,
Which jump on the table and tie up the knots.
Each giggle escapes as I trip on a shoe,
What a daring adventure for me and the crew!

The clock ticks in time with an unheard beat,
As echoes of laughter make life feel complete.
In this hidden realm where silliness thrives,
I toast to the joy that silently drives.

Retreat into Silence

A room with a view of a wall full of dishes,
They're silently waiting, fulfilling their wishes.
The chair plays a game of who'll sit down first,
While the clock, quite the jokester, loves to burst.

A tangle of yarn, oh the stories it tells,
Of cats who achieve their magical spells.
With humor so sly, the crumbs start to dance,
As I chuckle away at my disorganized trance.

In the still of the air, a spider spins lace,
Crafting fine webs in this peculiar place.
I sip on my drink, which spills down my shirt,
A little surge of laughter, amidst the dessert.

So here in this haven where silence is loud,
I find all my quirks wrapped in a cloud.
Joy sneaks in quietly, and I revel in bliss,
Grateful for moments that I wouldn't miss.

Calm Between the Noise

Amidst whirring gadgets and clattering cups,
The peaceful eek of roaches, oh, how they sup.
I tiptoe around, trying not to disturb,
The chaos that welcomes me, truly absurd!

Chairs squeak their secrets, and pillows all sigh,
While socks roll their eyes as they tumble on by.
The fridge hums a tune of forgotten delights,
In the calm between noise, I reach new heights.

Here laughter collides with the hum of the air,
As I trip on a dream that seems awkwardly fair.
I bend down to laugh at the dust bunnies' waltz,
Finding joy in this chaos, all my little faults.

So here's to the oddness that life tends to share,
In this funny retreat, I'm blissfully aware.
With each silly moment joining the parade,
This calm midst the noise is where I've been made.

Reflective Reverie

In corners deep, a cat snores loud,
With dreams of fish and a bustling crowd.
A chair creaks softly, and dust bunnies dance,
While socks play hide-and-seek in a trance.

The clock ticks slow, it seems to tease,
As tea leaves swirl with utmost ease.
The wallpaper grins, it's seen it all,
A silent witness to each giggle and fall.

A book lies open, pages ajar,
Where heroes dwell, both near and far.
The lamp flickers, casting shadows wide,
While laughter echoes, the heart's true guide.

Outside the window, the squirrels conspire,
To stage a heist with needless desire.
Yet inside these walls, with whimsy we play,
A refuge for laughter, come what may.

Vale of Stillness

In a nook where the quiet opinions parade,
The spoons debate all the tea they've made.
An old shoe grumbles about the walk,
While mismatched buttons begin to talk.

Bright cushions gossip, their seams all frayed,
As the golden retriever dreams of a raid.
The clock on the wall has lost its race,
Telling stories of time in a sleepy embrace.

A mirror reflects all the fun that went 'round,
With decades of squabbles and laughter profound.
The fridge hums a melody, soft and sweet,
While vegetables plot a daring escape from heat.

In this vale of echoes, the gnomes have a plan,
To talk about life while peer-pressured by a fan.
It's a gathering here, where silliness reigns,
Where even the napkins make attempts at refrains.

Tides of Tranquil Thought

A lazy dog sprawls in the warm sunbeam,
Dreaming of treats and a sandwich theme.
While inside a rug tickles toes in glee,
As plants whisper secrets, just between me.

The sink hums softly, like a soothing tune,
While cupcakes plot under the light of the moon.
A pair of old shoes squeak out a song,
As socks dance the night, where do they belong?

The tea pot spills tales of a world unseen,
Where pots and pans can host a cuisine.
In this flowing tide, each thought is a wave,
That swirls with laughter and joy to save.

As objects conspire in the light of the day,
With funny ambitions, in their quirky way.
This place of calm is spun with delight,
Where silliness bubbles, oh what a sight!

Escape into Serenity

An empty chair whispers, 'Come sit for a while,'
Where books hug each other and unwind with a smile.
The teacups play tag, with saucers as shields,
In the echoes of laughter, mischief is revealed.

A clock with no hands spins tales of the past,
While a jigsaw puzzle pretends it's a cast.
The feathers from pillows float softly above,
Each one a reminder of laughter and love.

As the walls share secrets in colors so bright,
A sneaky old curtain steals glimpses of light.
Beneath those bright skies, the imagination flows,
In the quiet of corners, blissfully it grows.

An escape to this haven where echoes speak loud,
We share silly dreams with the furniture proud.
In laughter, we find that serenity's near,
In this whimsical space, where joy does appear.

The Art of Listening to Silence

In corners where whispers play,
An echo of thoughts where shadows sway,
A chair sits still, its secret known,
It listens close, but feels all alone.

The clock ticks loud, yet time stands still,
The dust dances, with utmost thrill,
A mug of tea wears a sleepy grin,
As it contemplates where to begin.

A cat sprawls across the wooden floor,
Dreaming of fish, and perhaps some more,
He hears the silence, with a twitching ear,
Wondering why no one will appear.

With a creak, the floorboards join the chat,
They speak of the cat or maybe a rat,
In this quiet place, humor does thrive,
Nonsense and laughter, oh how they jive!

In the Embrace of Stillness

In a room where time seems to pause,
The couch makes jokes without a cause,
It sighs and stretches, loves the refrain,
Of sunlight filtering through the rain.

The potted plant shakes a tiny leaf,
Whispering secrets, a comic relief,
Staying quiet is its greatest art,
While plotting how to steal a heart.

Windows giggle as breezes pass,
Fluttering curtains have quite the sass,
They swish and swirl in playful delight,
Gathering stories of day and night.

Even the silence dons a bright mask,
Filling the air with a hilarious task,
To hear the laughter of the unseen,
In the embrace where the calm convenes!

Faded Pages and Forgotten Tales

Old books stacked high, a musty smell,
Whispering stories they long to tell,
Their pages faded, yet spirits bright,
Each tale a chuckle, a pure delight.

The bookmarks gather dust like the rest,
Trying to remember who read them best,
An owl hoots softly from atop the shelf,
Mumbling about books, and needing help.

With every turn, a ghostly cheer,
In corners where laughter lingers near,
The words tumble forth, giggles abound,
In pages turned, mirth can be found.

Each spine cracked open invites a grin,
As dust motes swirl in a whimsical spin,
Forgotten tales with a playful twist,
In the quiet where stories exist!

A Symphony of Subdued Light

In the glow of dusk, shadows prance,
They play a tune, oh what a dance!
A lamp winks cheerfully by the wall,
Playing spotlight on nothing at all.

The ceiling hums a gentle refrain,
A serenade of laughter, not pain,
While curtains sway like they know a joke,
In a symphony, nobody spoke.

The furniture sighs with every creak,
Riddled with secrets, they never speak,
But in the silence, they beam with cheer,
As if the light knows all that's dear.

Each flicker, a chuckle, each shadow, a sigh,
Lighting the room as the minutes fly by,
In this wonderland of subdued delight,
Even silence knows how to be light!

The Comfort of Open Windows

A gentle breeze whispers through,
I hope it carries gossip too.
The curtains dance in silly twirls,
As outside life unfurls its swirls.

The cat's gaze sharp, a feathery thief,
Chasing shadows, feeling no grief.
Birds tweet tunes we've never heard,
As if to mock a sleepy word.

Dust bunnies roll like playful pets,
Competing for dust-mite best bets.
The sun shines gold on every face,
In this light-hearted, silly space.

With laughter stuck in every crack,
I find my way, I won't look back.
These open windows, what a sight,
Make cozy moments feel just right.

Memories Wrapped in Cotton

Old quilts draped like silly monsters,
Hiding treasures, and fond blunders.
The laughs we shared, tucked in each seam,
A cozy hug, a sleepy dream.

Grandma's cookies with sprinkles bright,
Turn memories into a delight.
Sticky fingers, chocolate on nose,
Moments like these, who really knows?

The teddy bear still guards my dreams,
With secrets wrapped in giggly schemes.
Under this soft and spongy quilt,
Is where all the cherished smiles are built.

Fuzzy socks dance on the floor,
To melodies we can't ignore.
In this haven of cotton embrace,
We spin our tales at a gentle pace.

Traces of Laughter in Quiet Rooms

Cracks in the wall hold whispers spry,
Echoes of giggles that won't die.
A ghost of a joke still stays alive,
In corners where silly spirits thrive.

Cushions may hide, a secret or two,
Like ticklish toes, they chuckle too.
The clock laughs loudly at time's slow creep,
While laughter bounces, a joyful leap.

Glimmers of fun in a dusty book,
That tells of adventures for which we took.
Every shelf holds a snapshot of cheer,
Whispers of joy ringing loud and clear.

These quiet rooms, a curious blend,
Of solemn thoughts and jokes that bend.
In every shadow, a grinning face,
Reminding us of this silly space.

Sheltered from the Storm

Pitter patter plays on the roof,
As raindrops giggle, a playful goof.
Inside, we hide with cups of tea,
And talk of where the cat could be.

Lightning flashes, the bulbs will wane,
Yet our laughter outshines the rain.
Blankets piled high, a fort we make,
A castle formed from cookies and cake.

The storm may roar, but so do we,
As thunder hums a silly spree.
The walls might shake, but we just grin,
In laughter's warmth, we feel the win.

So here we stay, safe from the fright,
With stories spun till the morning light.
Let the tempest rage and swirl with force,
We'll ride it out with laughter's course.

Unseen Landscapes of Thought

In corners dust bunnies play,
They host debates about the day.
With cups of tea and crumpets too,
They laugh at me, what can I do?

A fridge hums songs of old, it seems,
Whispering secrets of my dreams.
I tiptoe past, it winks in glee,
It knows my snacks, oh woe is me!

Pillows gather for a chat,
Discussing all that I have at.
They gossip low, a quite sly crew,
Plotting if I'll take a snooze or two.

In these realms of gentle jest,
Where thoughts can frolic like a guest.
Each shadow dances, each beam beams bright,
In this haven, oh what a sight!

Stillness Speaks

The clock ticks lightly on the wall,
It whispers secrets, a silent call.
With every tick, a giggle it spills,
As it counts down my pointless thrills.

A vase of flowers, quite aloof,
Tells tales of past with a haughty poof.
Petals rustle, dancers in breeze,
Daring me to join, oh if you please!

Cobwebs stretch like lazy cats,
Carefree in corners, wearing hats.
They've trapped some dreams from years before,
Each thread a memory, and maybe more.

Stillness hums a playful tune,
Underneath the watchful moon.
In this space, where silence grows,
Laughter blooms, and joy bestows!

The Calm Within My Walls

Within these walls of gentle pause,
My heart finds rhythm, a playful cause.
The sofa sighs with every sit,
As I dive in, the cushions fit.

Curtains flutter like flags in flight,
Daring the sun to stay for a night.
They wink at me, mischievous in cheer,
Inviting laughter to hang near.

A teapot whistles a song so sweet,
Inviting chaos with a tea-time treat.
I tune in close, as laughter peals,
In this calm, the fun reveals.

Here inside, where whispers roam,
I craft a world that feels like home.
Each moment swirls with whimsy bright,
In this haven, things feel just right!

Resounding Quietude

In the stillness, echoes play,
A plushy bear joins in the fray.
Soft laughter creeps from shadows deep,
As secrets stir from quiet sleep.

Books lean close and share a grin,
Their pages flip, inviting in.
With tales of laughter, joy unfolds,
Each line a giggle, every word bold.

Sunbeams dance on polished floors,
As they jive through open doors.
Dust mites boogie to the light,
In this stillness, all feels right.

Oh how lovely the quiet hum,
Where silly thoughts and dreams do come.
In this space, joy finds its way,
Where laughter lives — come, let's play!

Lap of Inner Peace

In a corner, a cat takes a snooze,
While the goldfish dreams of ocean blues.
A couch of cushions, fluff piled high,
Squeaky toys squeal, under pillow sky.

Tea stains the table, a curious mess,
Muffins gone missing, it's anyone's guess.
Laughter erupts as we bump our heads,
In this joy-filled realm where silliness spreads.

Clouds of laughter float in the room,
While socks celebrate their hidden gloom.
Cookies declare it's party time,
In this space of clumsy rhyme.

And when night falls, the stars come to play,
Even the moon joins the frolicsome fray.
A bed of pillows, where dreams all collide,
In this strange oasis, we giggle and hide.

Sanctuary of Solitude

A chair that creaks with every thought,
Where peace is served with each cup bought.
In corners, potted plants softly smile,
Reminding me to pause, if just for a while.

The kettle whistles, a loud alarm,
But in this bubble, it feels like a charm.
Socks on the floor have thrown a parade,
Spilling laughter in every escapade.

A cat on the windowsill eyes the street,
Watching squirrels in their dance of deceit.
While I sip tea, it's all just a game,
In this space where life plays its own name.

Quiet giggles behind each door,
As thoughts glide by, who could ask for more?
Between these four walls, serenity hums,
With small joys resting, like kingdom crumbs.

Melodies of Musing

Tunes of sunlight dance on the walls,
While socks engage in their own waltz calls.
A duck quacks loudly, a guest in my dream,
Floating through thoughts like a whimsical stream.

A teapot sings, its whistle so bright,
Competing with crickets who chirp at night.
My notebook chuckles with doodles and jots,
Filling these pages with happy little thoughts.

In this symphony of laughter and grace,
A cookie crumbles, it can't keep pace.
Pages flip gently as breezes take hold,
Whispering secrets of stories untold.

The sun dips down, shadows start to sway,
While musings expand, like a playful ballet.
Each note a treasure, a heartfelt embrace,
In melodies crafted within this space.

Shadows of Reflection

In the dim light, where giggles abide,
Mirrors flicker, as shadows collide.
A plant taps its foot to an unknown beat,
While I trip over thoughts, a clumsy repeat.

Here, every glance tells a joke or two,
While scribbles on pads join the hullabaloo.
A dust bunny waltzes across the floor,
As I laugh and dance with this charming decor.

Pillows conspire to hide me away,
As footsie tournaments brighten the day.
In these reflections, the world seems so small,
With jokes flying high like an aerial ball.

I write my secrets, a comedy gold,
Where thoughts of levity warm up the cold.
In this reflective dance, joy takes its chance,
And shadows join in for a nonsensical prance.

Solitude's Embrace

In a room where whispers giggle,
Socks debate on how to wriggle.
Chairs conspire, oh what a scene,
The cat's the queen, or so it seems.

Dust bunnies dance with glee,
Holding meetings underneath the spree.
A light bulb flickers, plays a game,
While the clock ticks, never the same.

Naps are taken on the floor,
Cushions plot to open a door.
Tea cups gather, stories to mold,
In this space, fun never grows old.

Giggles float in each cozy nook,
Spiders weave tales in a book.
Pillows pillow fight at noon,
In solitude, life's a cartoon.

Echoes of the Heart

A mirror laughs at my surprise,
As my slippers play hide-and-seek guise.
Echoes bounce around the room,
Mimicking my dance, like an old cartoon.

Walls whisper secrets, oh so bold,
Telling tales of socks gone cold.
The fridge hums in a cheeky tone,
Offering leftovers, like a throne.

Chasing shadows, a curious game,
Each twist and turn, never the same.
I trip over thoughts, they give a cheer,
In this playful space, I have no fear.

Light streams in through cracks in the shade,
Creating a stage, an impromptu parade.
With laughter echoing, heart feels bright,
In the solitude, joy takes flight.

Voyage to the Inner Self

Set sail on a sea of thought,
With rubber ducks, not a single yacht.
Navigating dreams, oh what a trip,
Each wave a giggle, not a blip.

Compass points to the ice cream stand,
Map sketched out with a crayon hand.
Arriving at shores of cozy snacks,
Where cookies await, in little packs.

Clouds are pillows, drifting about,
Muffins cheer, "Come join the rout!"
The ocean whispers in sneaky tones,
Making rocks feel like weathered stones.

In this voyage, I'm never alone,
With funny fish singing every tone.
The hull of joy simply won't sink,
In the quiet, laughter's the link.

Reflection on Still Ground

In the stillness, a dance is made,
Beans sprout legs, a little parade.
Mirrors crack jokes, light up the gloom,
While old chairs rumble, shaking the room.

Puddles laugh under shoes that slip,
Pine cones applaud, as I flip and skip.
A gentle breeze teases my hair,
Tickling the silence, everywhere.

Footprints gather to share their tales,
As crickets play some merry scales.
Reflections chuckle on the ground,
In solitude's grip, joy is found.

With each glance in the glass so clear,
I see a party that's always near.
In this stillness, let laughter swell,
Quiet's a riot, can't you tell?

Driftwood of Thought

Waves crash softly, thoughts afloat,
A rubber duck flags down a boat.
Naps on the porch, snacks on the side,
Driftwood dreams gently collide.

Socks in the breeze, a dance on the line,
Laughter echoes, a sun-soaked shrine.
Jellybeans tumble, they roll and they fall,
Gathering thoughts, we'll share them all.

Whispering winds play tricks on my brain,
While squirrels collect secrets like candy from rain.
The sun tickles shadows, a playful tease,
Every silly thought is a breeze with ease.

In the realm of the ridiculous and sweet,
Time gives its nod, making joy complete.
Here in the soft, we ponder and plot,
Driftwood of thought, an unforeseen lot.

A Stronghold of Silence

In this castle of quiet, a chortle takes flight,
Where whispers of giggles flee into the night.
The corners are cozy, the cushions are plump,
Curiosity stirs, giving boredom a thump.

Tea cups clatter, we raise a clink,
Bigfoot's a friend, or so we think.
Imaginary feasts with crumbs of delight,
A fortress of silence, we conquer the night.

Echoes of laughter, like shadows they fling,
Whiskers on kittens wearing crowns to bling.
Hiding from seriousness, running for fun,
Life in this haven is never outdone.

So here we will stay, and let worries slide,
A stronghold of silence where silliness bides.
Each giggle a treasure, each punchline a prize,
In this fortress of fun, we all improvise.

Interlude in the Calm

Midday sun sprawls, like cats in a heap,
A chicken rebounds, or is it a sheep?
Tales of the absurd float softly like mist,
In this interlude, we can't help but twist.

A cup of mischief, poured with a grin,
Tango of whimsy, let the frolics begin.
Clouds wearing hats, so puffy and round,
In this calm interlude, our laughs resound.

Cacti with googly eyes, oh what a sight!
Dancing in shadows, playing all night.
Mirth bubbles up, and time takes a pause,
Finding delight in the silliest cause.

So let's raise a cheer for bumbles and blunders,
Each pause in the calm, the universe wanders.
Here's to the laughter, the jesters, the throng,
In this little respite, we all belong.

Threads of Reflection

Stitching together the pieces we find,
Threads of reflection, twirling in mind.
Circus of thoughts in a wild parade,
Each moment a detail, in hues not yet made.

Wobbling teacups, they echo the fun,
Dance across tables, oh what have we spun?
Jigsaw of giggles, putting us near,
In threads of reflection, we cheer and we leer.

The sun slips away, in playful retreat,
Cracks in the laughter, unable to beat.
Wrapping our stories in yarns of delight,
Each thread a reminder, of joy in the night.

In this playful tapestry, we thread and we weave,
Filling up pockets with dreams to believe.
So let's knot our worries, spin tales to confound,
In threads of reflection, silliness found.

Beneath the Stillness

In the corner, a cat naps tight,
Dreaming of fish in a sunbeam light.
Creak of the floor, it's just a chair,
Or is it a ghost with a banjo to share?

Dust bunnies dance in the golden sun,
All of them plotting, oh what a fun run!
A sock on the shelf with a grin so wide,
Might just be hiding a magician inside.

Cradle of Memories

Old photos smile with a wink and a nod,
Uncle Joe's wig still looks quite odd.
Stories spill out from the walls all around,
Of mishaps and mayhem, silliness found.

A tea set once used for a grand wizard's brew,
Now holds stale cookies and an old shoe.
Echoes of laughter, a ghostly delight,
In a home that remembers both day and night.

Lullabies of the Mind

The clock ticks a tune, with a tickle and tease,
While the fridge hums softly as if it's at ease.
Cozy corners whisper in secrets and sighs,
Where imaginations wander, with curious eyes.

Socks held hostage, a strange little game,
That pair on the shelf? They're always to blame!
A chair that squeaks like a baby whale's song,
Utters its thoughts, 'Is this where I belong?'

Still Waters Run Deep

In a puddle, a frog strikes a thoughtful pose,
Contemplating life, while munching on hose.
Bubbles of laughter float up through the air,
As the goldfish debates with the cat in despair.

The curtains sway gently, with secrets they keep,
While ants host a party, a wacky heap.
The light dances twinkling on dusty old shelves,
Where even the books chuckle at themselves.

Chamber of the Unsaid

In a room where thoughts just roam,
Leftovers of words begin to foam.
A sock whispers secrets to a shoe,
While dust bunnies dance—who knew?

The clock ticks loud, it seems to jest,
Tick-tock jokes, it's quite the pest.
Chairs giggle under the old oak tree,
As they plot a rebellion, just wait and see.

Mirrors reflect a cheeky smirk,
Elusive echoes of the quirky work.
Where shadows play hide-and-seek at noon,
And wiseguys shine like a silver spoon.

So come and join this wacky crew,
In the chamber of things we never knew.
Stuffy with laughter, it won't be bland,
A riotous giggle fest, oh so grand!

Reflections in a Quiet Stream

Bubbles pop like tiny laughs,
As fish tell jokes from their watery halves.
A pebble named Gus grins at the scene,
He's the funniest rock you've ever seen.

The reeds sway gently, shimmying around,
While frogs share puns with a croaky sound.
Across the bank, a squirrel sips tea,
Complaining about how bumpy life can be.

Reflections ripple, distorting the truth,
A cat in a hat claims to be sleuth.
With each little wave, the giggles ensue,
As nature's stand-up show continues anew.

So sit by the stream, let laughter take flight,
In the gentle embraces of day and night.
The water holds stories, profound and yet light,
In reflections where joy takes center stage bright.

Celestial Whispers

Stars gather round for a cosmic chat,
Comets with mustaches, imagine that!
"Hey, did you hear about Mars' new hair?"
"Yeah, it's frizzier than a wild bear!"

The moon winks down with a silvery glee,
While meteors tease, "We're shooting VIP!"
Galaxies giggle, swirling around,
As laughter echoes in the vast sound.

Planets play tag in their dizzying race,
Uranus trails behind, just keeping pace.
Time zones joke, "Are we lost in a light?"
"Who cares!" quips Pluto, "We'll party tonight!"

In this realm where humor takes flight,
Even black holes pull a prank; what a sight!
So look up and smile at the sky's funny ways,
Where stardust shimmers and frolics all day.

Murmurs in the Air

Listen closely, can you hear the buzz?
The wind tells tales; yes, it surely does!
Clouds trade one-liners like seasoned pros,
While feathers fall laughing, oh how it goes!

A squirrel shouts, "Catch me if you can!"
While the breeze replies, "You don't stand a chance!"
Trees sway in rhythm, their leaves all shake,
Creating a ruckus, a playful quake.

Sunbeams play peek-a-boo with the ground,
Shadow puppets dance with nary a sound.
The air's alive with quips and romantic flair,
As whispers of joy swirl and dare.

Embrace the joy in the subtle stir,
In murmurs of laughter, let your heart purr.
For in every gust of wind that we share,
Are little moments of love in the air.

Shadows of Serenity

In a corner where socks like to hide,
And the cat sits with dubious pride.
Shadows dance, oh what a sight,
Whispers of laughter in the night.

The clock ticks off its silly tune,
As dust bunnies plan a grand monsoon.
With each creak, a giggle might chase,
The chaos wrapped in stillness' embrace.

Under the table, a sneeze will occur,
As a fly tries to go for a tour.
The curtains giggle, with each little breeze,
As they watch the antics of dust and cheese.

Oh, how the cushions start to conspire,
Forming a fort, a castle of fire.
In this stillness, true mirth will be found,
Where pure joy twirls, all around.

Hushed Moments

In the silence where whispers collide,
A sneaky soup pot takes a wide glide.
Spaghetti dreams and sauce on the wall,
Hushed moments tumble, ready to fall.

Rugrats giggle, with crumbs in their wake,
Planning to launch a grand birthday cake.
The microwave ding, oh what a prank,
As popcorn pops and spills from the flank.

A cat's stealth gives rise to a pounce,
Where the fishbowl sits, a watery bounce.
In quietude, a ruckus does bloom,
As socks and snacks play, sharing the room.

With each giggle wrapped in silence's cloak,
A bashful fart escapes, and they choke.
In hushed harmony, chaos resides,
Where laughter does wave, and joy collides.

Tranquil Corners

In a nook where old chairs seem to sigh,
The plants eavesdrop, oh my, oh my!
Each tick of the clock holds a tiny jest,
As time takes a break for a much-needed rest.

The teapot dances, it's quite a show,
While spoons start to giggle, don't you know?
In tranquil corners, the plights unfold,
Where even the pantry has stories untold.

A stray cookie crumb tells a tale so sweet,
Of adventures and mischief beneath little feet.
Each shadow whispers secrets no one will hear,
While the floorboards chuckle, full of good cheer.

What a circus, this calm little space,
With cushions in corners, the silliest place.
For in stillness, the absurd can still thrive,
With funny tales riding on the vibe.

Silent Reverie

In a dream where the kettle sings out loud,
And the broom takes a bow, oh so proud.
Silent reverie with a wink and a grin,
The universe chuckles, where antics begin.

The cushions are plotting a brave little scheme,
As they bounce on the sofa with a giggling beam.
A rogue radio hums the tune of the day,
While slippers conspire to frolic and play.

Dishes in stacks become towers so grand,
As they wobble and topple, a team unplanned.
In this place of quiet, so whimsically neat,
Even the ceiling fans tap their feet.

As shadows whisper and laughter takes flight,
In silent reverie, we dance through the night.
Every corner filled with nonsense and cheer,
Where the joy of the moment is crystal and clear.

Breaths of the Unseen

In corners where shadows dance and tease,
Whispers giggle through rustling leaves.
Dust bunnies hold a grand debate,
On whether to hop or just wait.

The curtains swish, they claim they're shy,
While the carpets chuckle, oh my, oh my!
A clock ticks backwards just for fun,
Saying, 'Time is a game, let's run!'

Mirrored faces make funny grins,
As the teapot spills its spicy sins.
Cats play chess with their own tails,
While a mouse narrates their funny fails.

Laughter echoes down the hall,
Echoes of tiny, comical brawls.
Here, every breath is a playful jest,
In this nook, we find true rest!

Gaze into the Void

Staring deep into the empty space,
Finding humor in a missing face.
The sofa wiggles, making a joke,
And the wallpaper starts to poke.

Light bulbs flicker like they know a secret,
Making shadows dance, oh what a feat!
The fridge hums a melodic tune,
While the spoons plot to make a cartoon.

Empty cups are planning a spree,
Pretending they're cups of herbal tea.
In this void, creativity births,
Silly thoughts float like gentle girths.

Gaze into nothing, find what's fun,
In silence, laughter has just begun.
Here in this space, joy takes a stand,
With the silliness of the mundane at hand!

The Art of Stillness

In the stillness, where giggles reside,
Pots and pans always seem to hide.
The kettle sings, a high-pitched tune,
While the forks tap their dance under the moon.

A squirrel knocks, trying to gain entry,
With a tumble and roll, so very gentry.
Silence is loud, in a most funny way,
Pillow fights echo, come out and play!

The chairs think they're royalty of the room,
While the cushions sigh, making more gloom.
Yet laughter finds its way through tight seams,
Where whispers and chuckles fulfill their dreams.

Stillness brings a playful twist,
A comedy show we can't resist.
In this pause, we craft the bizarre,
Creating joy that shines like a star!

Bonds Beyond Words

In the silence, friends collide with glee,
Bonds formed among shadows, can't you see?
A cracker jokes that it's too cheesy,
While the jam sighs, feeling quite breezy.

The curtains gossip with a little flair,
As the fridge whispers, 'I've got cold air!'
Together, they weave stories so bright,
Of bread that dreamed it could take flight.

In every chuckle, a connection grows,
Like a plant sprouting from the garden hose.
Here, unspoken ties are neatly spun,
In laughter's embrace, we are all one.

Silent bonds create a lively scene,
Where every nudge and wink is seen.
In this mirthful gathering, hearts unite,
Crafting a masterpiece of sheer delight!

Reflections in Frosted Glass

In rooms where echoes play and leap,
A cat naps on an old heap.
The couch, a throne for lazy kings,
Where laughter dances on silly wings.

The fridge hums tunes of snacks galore,
While socks embark on a quest for more.
With every creak, the walls join in,
As secrets slip on a pillow thin.

Old photos wink from frames of gold,
Tales of mishaps that never get old.
A mirror grins back with a sly little crack,
Saying, "Today, let's never look back!"

In this haven where giggles blend,
The mischievous spirits know no end.
Here, moments hang like clothes on a line,
In the chill of humor, forever entwined.

Serenity's Breath in Every Nook

Amidst the cushions, a creaky chair,
Whispers secrets of quiet flair.
With every sip of tea so warm,
A rubber duck adds to the charm.

The clock ticks slow, each second grins,
At socks that played hide-and-seek wins.
A fern dreams of being a tall palm tree,
As laughter bubbles like a soft tea spree.

In the corner, an old broom sighs,
While teddy bears plot their surprise.
The dust settles like gentle rain,
And tickles thoughts spun in playful chain.

Curtains sway to a silent tune,
A chair groans like an old cartoon.
In this snug nook where giggles drift,
Even stillness wraps in a cozy gift.

Veils of Dust and Dream

Beneath a veil of shimmering dust,
Lies a dreamer with an uproarious thrust.
The vacuum's curse lingers in the air,
While shadows tango without a care.

Cobwebs spin tales both strange and funny,
For laughter blooms like bright spring honey.
The chair looks back with a knowing stare,
"Why do we sit? Come, let's dance in the air!"

In a pocket of time, the old clock smirks,
Counting giggles and cheeky quirks.
A picture frame holds a jester's grin,
"Life's a game; let's dive right in!"

Through every corner, a chuckle springs,
Dusty memories wear invisible wings.
In this realm of whimsy and cheer,
Even sorrow gives a bright little sneer.

Candles Flicker in the Twilight

Candles sway with a dance tonight,
Casting shadows that giggle in fright.
The window whispers tales from afar,
As fireflies join in, a tiny bizarre.

On the table, snacks arrange in rows,
While nibbling mice put on their shows.
A grand feast for all, with crumbs galore,
As dreams unfurl in the flickering roar.

Each flame flickers with a playful tease,
Chasing laughter like leaves in the breeze.
The walls hum songs of forgotten fun,
As twilight giggles, "Oh, we've just begun!"

In this glow of warmth and delight,
Every shadow is a friend tonight.
With every wink, the candles sway,
In a carnival of dusk, we dance and play.

Veiling the Mind's Whirl

In corners snug, where whispers play,
Thoughts spin like tops, dance and sway.
A cat on a rug, a silent judge,
Declaring my chaos, won't budge.

With teacups stacked like Jenga dreams,
And laughter hiding in gentle streams.
I trip on a sock, the dog gives a glare,
This maze of my mind is quite a dare.

Each book on the shelf tells tales untold,
Of riddles and puzzles, each leaf of gold.
I search for wisdom in an old casserole,
Finding ideas like lost jelly rolls.

But in this chaos, I'm never alone,
A circus of thoughts that feel like home.
So weave me a tapestry, bright and absurd,
In the whirl of my mind, I happily stirred.

Enclave of Thought

A nook in the wall, where ideas collide,
With coffee and donuts, side by side.
Here puns are crafted like fine art,
Guarded by giggles and a quick-witted dart.

Papers pile high, a tower of cheer,
Each scribble a secret, a joke held dear.
In this enclave, all whimsy is found,
With laughter echoing, round and round.

My brain is a garden, weeds intertwining,
Yet flowers of humor are brightly shining.
An onion of thoughts, layer by layer,
Reveal a punchline that's truly a player.

But clarity stumbles on mismatched socks,
While I search for wisdom in tick-tock clocks.
So let's raise a toast to thoughts on the roam,
In this charming retreat, I'm never alone.

Solace in Shadows

In the shadows where giggles hide,
Thoughts bump and tumble, train wrecks collide.
The dust bunnies cheer for their favorite show,
A sock puppet quarrel, oh what a blow!

Under the table, snacks take their place,
I'm plotting a heist with a scone and some grace.
The curtains are twitching, the friends all decree,
This cozy chaos is blissfully free.

An echo of laughter, a slip on a shoe,
Chasing my thoughts like they're hiding from view.
In a realm of muddles, I lean to confide,
In the solace of shadows, my quirks coincide.

So here's to the whispers and unexpected cheers,
To the fun in the silence that soothes all my fears.
With whimsies that flutter like leaves racing by,
In my twisted little hideout, oh how I fly!

Quietude's Palette

With crayons of thoughts, I color the day,
In shades of absurd, I loiter and play.
A splash of mischief, a dab of delight,
My canvas of calm is a curious sight.

Squiggles and lines, they dance through my mind,
Creating a picture uncannily blind.
The colors are wild, the hues all askew,
In this quietude, laughter breaks through.

Paint spills like secrets on the floor,
Splashing the pet cat, she runs for the door.
A masterpiece born from the chaos I dwell,
In the quietest corners, I weave my own spell.

So invite me to ponder, to muse and to grin,
In this palette of nonsense, I'll revel within.
With each stroke of humor, I find more to see,
In my whimsical world, it's just you and me.

www.ingramcontent.com/pod-product-compliance
Lightning Source LLC
Chambersburg PA
CBHW070002300426
43661CB00141B/131